Financial Success

A Complete Guide to Building YOUR Wealth

RK Jack

Foreword

There are a million "Get Rich!" books out there. So, what makes mine unique? Simple—

Real-world experience.

The one commonality among the many financial books I have read is that most seem to want to instill their "one secret" to help you get rich quickly.

From my experience, though, there is only one secret to easy wealth: extreme luck.

Were you born to wealthy parents? Did you win the lottery? Have you stumbled into a niche in the market, or bought a stock or cryptocurrency that just happened to produce fabulous wealth?

No?

Then, let's look at how the rest of the 90% of us get "wealthy". The "one secret" to that?

Proper planning and dedicated execution of that plan over time—a *lot* of time.

One of my goals after retiring from the federal government was to write a financial self-help book that mattered to ordinary people—people like you and me. Those who say, "Skip avocado toast, make a budget and stick to it, or invest your latte money, and you will get rich!" are insulting and counterproductive.

How so?

I will give you a hint. It is nothing against those authors—having a budget and saving money *is* vital to financial success, but it just isn't ever going to be enough to succeed on that alone. Do research on how millionaires became that way (if they were not born into it). They didn't get there by investing $100 a month from not having lattes, while paying down their credit cards. No, they worked their way up to a higher income and invested money to have more significant amounts *years* and *decades* later. And, just like them, you can start now. Even if it is only one percent of your paycheck, start now!

Seriously, put this book down and submit the paperwork to have it withheld from your pay and deposited (pre-tax!) at work. If your employer doesn't have a retirement match—or even retirement contributions at all—then go to a brokerage firm (such as Fidelity© or Charles Shwabb©), open an IRA, and have your pre-tax paycheck deductions go to it.

Welcome back. If you did this one thing, my book has already been of great value to you.

I didn't start writing non-fiction to get rich. Unlike authors who seem to say the best way to get rich is to write self-help books, that is not why I wrote this. I want you to succeed, and I would love to hear directly from you on how your financial journey is evolving.

So why *did* I do it? Because I wish someone had been around to tell me the things I wrote in this book when I was young—someone to say to me that building wealth is a lifestyle and way of thinking. I would make mistakes, but if I did just a few things right, I could retire comfortably. And they are not "hard" things to do. They aren't easy either, but they are doable and will reward you as the years and decades go by as you *live* your life.

Throughout this book, I will discuss the financial advice of someone who has lived it. Take my successes and copy them (or add your own), and learn from my mistakes and failures. Many of those failures could have been huge successes! They also could have, just as easily, been *massive* failures. Hindsight is valuable, not to pick that "one stock" but to learn about the process. The biggest takeaway is to just invest in "index" stocks, like the S&P 500.

We will cover investing (and speculating) in individual stocks (a.k.a. companies) in a later chapter. That method of investing is not necessary for the plan, however.

So, without further ado, let's get started!

Contents

Introduction   xi

Part One
1. Planning For Success   3
2. Passive Income   7

Part Two
3. Youth   11
4. Young Adult   19
5. Career Adult   23
6. Late Career   27
7. Retirement   31

Part Three
8. The Big Three   35
9. Financial "Experts"   39
10. The Market   43
11. Afterlife   47
12. Pre-Birth   53
13. Generational Skipping   59

Part Four
Conclusion   67

Acknowledgments   71
About the Author   73
Connect with the Author   75
Appendix   77

FINANCIAL SUCCESS

Published by Horizon View Press LLC

Denver, CO

Copyright © 2025 by Russell Jack (RK Jack). All rights reserved.

BUS 050040 **BUSINESS & ECONOMICS** / Personal Finance / Retirement Planning

ISBN: 979-8-9900568-4-8

To everyone.

Indeed, if I can help make even one person attain Financial Success, then I consider this book a masterpiece.

Introduction

Hi, I am Russ, and it is truly a pleasure to "meet" you.

One thing that I noticed in many self-help books is the "talking like your friend" hype. Too many books should have an asterisk next to the title—one that says, "This is a paid advertisement for financial products that I get money from recommending to you."

That is not this book.

This book is about **your** journey and **your** success.

That is all that I am "selling you."

I want to tell you first what I don't sell: I don't sell financial products or false hope.

My only financial compensation comes from what someone paid me for this book, and I deliberately kept it inexpensive for this very reason. So, it is cheap unless you are reading it for free as a hand-me-down or from a library.

If so, kudos to you! Either way, I want you to get your time and money's worth.

However, I also want you to take what I have to offer

and build on it. I genuinely want you to succeed financially. My book should be a solid start (or continuation) of your financial learning, not the end. The road from now to your financial success is paved with one word: discipline.

Discipline is rooted in the Latin word "disciple," which means "a follower or student of something." So discipline is about self-control and studying, learning, and *following* the means to achieve a goal. It is something (in this case) that you are driven to do and that you follow through on, day after day. Yes, the word can also mean other things, such as punishment, but that is not the definition we are using.

I want you to continue to keep learning and strive for success.

You will experience setbacks and failures, unexpected life changes (or preferably planned ones), and surprises galore!

If you are dedicated to learning and *practicing* what you know, you will succeed. Faster or slower, it does not matter; if you are **committed** to creating your financial freedom, you will succeed!

This book idea has been in my head for decades.

I started my adult life poor, working full-time at $5 an hour (the federal minimum wage in 1991).

Sadly, it is still only $7.25 an hour.

The most crucial financial thing I did was work my way up in my career, and that "up" meant more significant and bigger paychecks.

Like almost everyone else, I had to work long and hard to get that hourly wage up. During that journey, I paid off debts, worked my butt off, learned how to make and save money, and read self-help books on becoming debt-free and financially successful. (I mention some additional reading suggestions on this topic in the appendix at the back of the book.)

Then, I took on new debts, made wise and dumb financial decisions, and eventually realized the ups and downs of a half-century of life. If you can be robotic in your choices and follow all sound financial advice to become wealthy nearly perfectly, I want to congratulate you!

And then ask, where were you built?

I have never met that perfect person and never will. The first "rule" of being human is you WILL screw up—over and over again. Your best-laid plans will get sidetracked by the unexpected or even just by your desires, especially when your "wants" take the lead.

Don't beat yourself up about it. Welcome to the other 99.99% of the world. Now, use those lessons and the lessons of others to stop making as many mistakes. Notice I did not say stop making them at all. You will still make mistakes, but learn and try your best not to do them again. This is where you start to succeed in your financial journey and your life. So, let's talk money—**your money.**

Finance is a fascinating field.

I have never seen a career where, statistically, the more you know about options trading, margins, and derivatives, the *worse* you perform on average, but the reason is simple:

Humans operate with emotion.

Try as hard as you want, but everyone I have met has done it. And the more "options" a trader has, the worse they seem to do, on average. Now, if you have a good, long-term track record and want to do this type of trading (after maxing out your retirement funding), then go ahead.

Just realize most of you (me included, by the way) will not beat the S&P 500 over 10+ years of individual investing. And since this book is about *you* in 10+ years, I can (based on experience) tell you to just "set it and forget it" to come out of your paycheck. Most of us are (or were) wage earners. If you are self-employed, the same "rules" of my book apply, but you need to balance the needs of your business with your long-term investment goals.

I want to tell you a little more about myself, just to give you a reference point and a reason to consider my advice and experiences. Why? Because you should *always* consider the source of your information.

I worked a thirty-plus-year "career" and am now financially successful.

Why the quotes? Because it took me almost eight years to get hired as a police officer with the federal government. During those years, I was a Military Police Army National Guardsman (enlisted first, then later as an officer). I attended college and worked dispatch and armed security jobs until I achieved my goal of becoming a police officer at 26. From there, it was another five years until I became a federal agent at 31. Then, just over 20 more years until I retired at 51. I have over twenty-five years with the federal government, but it took almost eight more years of work before that. Before I really "started" my federal career.

It took an *enormous* amount of time and effort to get into my field and to progress upward. That is normal and OK, and if you can do it faster with advanced degrees or just good ole' connections or luck, good for you! But that is not most of us.

Everyone wants to know the easy way.

As we discussed, unless you are fortunate enough to have received intergenerational wealth or win the lottery, you will most likely have to work for it.

I now have a net worth of $500k+.

But, Russ, that isn't enough to retire, is it?

Here's the thing: the goal of financial success is not a huge bank account; it is passive income, wherever that comes from—in my case, a pension. If you are not in a career that has one, and most do not, you may need more wealth than this if it is your only source.

You should examine how to minimize your debts and achieve sufficient passive income so you never have to work again. My only debt is my condo mortgage, and ideally, I would not have that either. Once more, I am sharing both my successes and my failures. I am not concealing my finances from you. Other authors may present a more optimistic view, but I want you to see a true example of a financial life, flaws and all.

No, I am not a millionaire, nor am I a "financial professional". I studied economics at the University of Colorado at Denver and have always loved learning about money and finance. I have been a micro-stock trader and even traded "regular" individual stocks. I did well but underperformed the S&P 500.

A government pension that I earned from over 25 years in the federal government allows me to retire at this age. Without that, I would need more of a nest egg to provide the income I need to be financially successful.

Why do I tell you this?

One thing I have lived by is that mentors or role models should lead by example. A big part of that is sharing not just success and what went well but also failures and what went poorly, especially the times you failed on the way to eventual success.

If you are training to become more fit and you are with a personal trainer who is out of shape, weak, and eats candy bars in front of you, should you listen to them?

No, you should not.

Don't listen to their "advice," even if they have a Ph.D. in nutrition and exercise physiology.

Why not?

Because you should only listen to advice from those who have actually *achieved* what you are looking for, and "practice what they preach". Of course, if they have related degrees or certificates, all the better.

What about me then? Why listen to me if I am not a millionaire or a certified financial planner?

Simple, because I am financially independent, retired, and successful, and I achieved all of these things at 51 years old. And that is why you are reading this book: to learn from me, the good and the bad decisions I have made. Then you read more books and watch and learn from others.

Go ahead and read the advice of "financial experts". If it is sound, incorporate it. Many of them have great ideas and plans, but unless they are already living proof of your desired goal, it is theoretical knowledge only. They should be a living example of what they preach and be willing to share how they got there. Then it is actual, real-world advice.

However, few of them have actually achieved what they preach.

Many of those author "experts" I have read over the years were not there yet either.

Of the few who were, many didn't achieve financial freedom on their own without the help of intergenerational wealth (a.k.a. inheritance or "gifts" to assist them). I am not taking anything away from their advice; much of it is well-researched and thought out. However, few authors have "made it" to financial freedom, and those who have are usually in their 50s or older. Amassing wealth takes time.

That is what makes me an "informal expert": the fact that I not only made it to my financial success, but also because I do read the other books, just like you.

Knowledge is power, but only when it is used.

If I, or other authors and role models, can save you even one big money mistake or help you to save more, then this book (and theirs) was a success!

"But others have achieved more than you in less time," you may say.

True. That leads me to an important life lesson—

One thing I had to learn the hard way is that my goal of success was not what I initially thought it was. Is a million dollars the real goal, like I had first planned? Or is it financial independence?

It is financial independence.

Don't get me wrong; achieving this independence requires money and a lot of it.

Money equals freedom.

But you have to live your life too!

The key to success in any endeavor is having a basic plan—one that can change over time but has solid fundamentals. So, to be financially successful, let's get started!

First, you must achieve a higher income. It doesn't have to be six figures (although that does not hurt), but it needs to be high enough to cover your lifestyle (including debt payments) and provide the money for your investments.

"Yeah, sure, must be nice!" you may say.

Bear with me...

No, you probably won't have this level of income in your first job or even your second, but you must make a plan to get there. I am not recommending a specific career, nor should anyone else.

This is your life we are talking about!

Your prime earning years will span decades, and your life dreams are part of having a fulfilling life. Don't *ever* make it all about money! The twenty to thirty years (or more) you spend working *is your life*. And a significantly big chunk of it!

You can live it well and still become wealthier each year.

Anyone who tells you that their method (including mine) is the only "guaranteed" method to lead you to success is selling you something. My book also isn't a guarantee because there are no guarantees in life, but there are proven actions you can take to help you achieve success (or failure), and a significant part of that is avoiding major financial mistakes.

Like the mistakes I have made! Just like *everyone* does.

Achieving financial success is a process. Does anyone think a professional athlete never gets hurt or sick or fails to place in a contest? Failure is part of success; we learn from our mistakes. The bigger the mistake, the more we learn.

What is my point? Those "money mistakes" are money you lose *forever* that could have been invested to make "future you" wealthier! You will still make those mistakes, but this book will help you make fewer of them or at least minimize the "damage" to your future wealth.

So... why not learn from others (like me) about those successes and failures? That way, you can "learn your lesson" without making those expensive mistakes!

Part of my planning for this book is to break this book down into the sections of your life. For many, your financial journey may be "ahead" or "behind" at different stages of your life. That is normal and OK.

I am simply telling you what I have learned and experienced (including what I have learned from others) to lead you down the road to success. Your successes and achievements will give you that on your own, but following the advice of others to avoid financial mistakes will help you to achieve that more efficiently and cost you almost nothing in return.

This is about so much more than just what you learn from me.

Learn from the successful role models who have accomplished what you want to achieve, from their successes and their failures. That brings me back to the most straightforward and most complex word you will ever read—

Discipline.

There are many meaning for this word. I know we touched on it during the foreword section, but it is so vital that we are going to go into even more detail about it. The meanings of discipline we are concentrating on are the ones dealing with two things:

1) The discipline of self-control: The ability to work and/or behave in a controlled manner, often following standards or rules. The root word is disciple: A follower or pupil of any teacher or school—someone dedicated to following a proscribed set of beliefs. Yes, these are paraphrased from the actual definitions you can look up. But once you are committed to a goal and truly dedicated, you will achieve it.

A proper plan plus effort over time equals success. It is indeed that simple, yet it remains quite challenging to actually achieve.

You are going to learn to be a disciple of your financial independence. You will learn, and keep learning, ways to accumulate wealth and passive income while eliminating debts. This "schooling" never stops. You must always strive to learn more. This is more than a mere hobby now; this is a core interest for you! So, what is a "Core Interest"?

2) Discipline as a "Core Interest": A core interest is something you do on a regular and recurrent basis. These are the things that you will do up to, and possibly even beyond, retirement. If you do something occasionally or rarely and it isn't something you are "into" and don't want to invest substantial time, money, and effort on (and learn

about), then that is a hobby, not a core interest. It's not a bad thing; just know the difference. Your efforts to learn and practice increasing your net worth (wealth) and passive income will take this level of commitment, but it will be worth it.

Either way, your occasional latte, avocado toast, or tiny purchase will not prevent you from reaching financial success.

Be pound-wise and penny-foolish to your heart's content.

I look back over the "smart" financial decisions I have made—and the "dumb" ones. Why the quotation marks? Because some "smart" decisions weren't, and some "dumb" decisions weren't.

Here is an example of an expensive hobby I enjoyed for decades: I loved performance cars and motorcycles. That hobby is a "dumb" financial decision, for sure. But I loved being a good driver! As a former soldier and law enforcement officer, I used those skills on duty. But did I need to buy expensive cars and motorcycles? No, I did not.

What if I had planned my "dumb" decision better?

Instead of having 20+ cars and 10+ motorcycles throughout my life, what if I had planned milestones of achievement for each? Such as "only one every ten years" or "if I achieve 'X,' then I can get 'Y'"; I would still have enjoyed the vehicles. In fact, I would have enjoyed them *more*.

Everyone knows about delayed gratification, but it really works! It makes you happier than getting what you want *right now*.

Many (most) of my vehicles were bought on credit.

I noticed something interesting, looking back at my "purchases." The motorcycles and cars that I actually **owned** (paid in full), I enjoyed more and kept longer than the ones I financed. This told me something after looking back over decades of life—enjoy what you have, not pining for what others have that you don't. There are always better, flashier, faster, larger, more expensive, etc., versions of whatever you have. There is no contest, not really. In the end, your wealth and happiness will be determined by your mind—train it to enjoy the value in something, not just the never-ending "hamster wheel" of always trying to have the best and greatest "things".

This proven methodology of achieving goals (or wealth or anything important) was drilled into me as a US Army officer—it is the "Seven Ps" concept:

Proper prior planning prevents piss poor performance.

Plan essential things in life; don't just do them. This is especially true when it comes to passive investing. This is money from your gross income into tax-deferred IRAs, 401ks, After-tax money into Roth IRAs, and other retirement accounts. It also applies to when (and whether) you buy something expensive.

First, and best, is not to have expensive hobbies at all.

For example, if you like video games, drive your virtual (and free) "six-figure car" there for only the cost of a video game. Then, buy a comfortable and reliable vehicle for transportation. You could even splurge on a really nice gaming/home-theater chair...

But, if, like me, you are driven (pun intended) to have an expensive hobby, at least plan it out. My favorite cars and motorcycles were all the ones I actually owned outright. A lot of fun is lost if you are working your butt off to afford a payment. But here is the interesting thing—my favorite motorcycle I drove for over a decade. It was paid for, and I enjoyed it more because I didn't have a loan payment.

We don't have to have the latest and greatest; society's (and corporate America's) goal is to make you spend as much money as possible, mostly just to have the best and newest "things" to impress those around you.

Don't fall for it like I did, like most people do.

Be an "intellectual minimalist".

Oh, and those people you are "impressing"? The biggest impression my co-workers actually had of me and my vehicles was how much money I kept losing, going from one shiny thing to the next. Don't worry about how others think of you by what you own (or rent/lease/mortgage). Being a good person to others doesn't cost money and will impress them far more. When you can take care of and make life better for those you love and others, I think we can agree that it is a much better "impression" to leave than what car you drove.

You can have things, just make sure each is paid for (not on credit) and that each is something you truly do get great utility or joy out of. Consider what it costs to use after it is paid for, also! Cars, boats, planes, time-shares, homes—all come with ongoing and never-ending costs, even *after* they are "paid for." You want to take a thorough look at these things before deciding if you want them. Unless you really get the joy from the money you are spending, skip them and get something you don't have to keep paying on for as long as you own it. Speaking of things—

The amount of "things" Americans accumulate is staggering!

If you give away (possibly for a tax write-off or even sell) all the things you don't really use, you will be amazed at just how much stuff you buy and then get rid of, just to replace it again later with even *more* things you also don't really cherish at all.

Another life lesson is this: always go forward. The past is over and gone. Sure, learn from your mistakes. But even better, and what this book is about, is learning from *other* people's mistakes—that way, you don't pay for them! This is true whether you are reading this at 10 years old or 80 years old.

Also, when you buy something, you should plan on keeping it (whatever *it* is) for a while. If it isn't quality enough to last, don't buy it at all. The same is valid for buying individual stocks, but that is a later chapter (and something you don't have to do at all—unless you want to).

In this book, we will break your life into stages, which will help us with planning. Unless you are born with a gem-encrusted silver spoon in your mouth (in which case, you are probably not reading this right now), you will have to earn your financial independence, quite literally.

Your wealth is the financially valuable things you own minus your debts—this is your Net Asset Value (NAV). In the grotesquely capitalist country of the United States of America (where I currently reside), people are judged by this. Remember, though, it is just a number, albeit an enormously important one.

You want a high NAV!

But you are not doing it to impress your neighbors and the Joneses—no one walks around with their NAV score scrolling on their forehead. No, people often judge your "perceived" wealth.

Let's look at two examples of "future you".

In the first example, you follow the lead of the multi-billion-dollar consumerism industry's "lifestyle fashion" version of yourself. Most of us followed this example or were heavily influenced by it—me included.

One that you will now avoid.

In the future, you will have arrived at a higher income. You will live in your own home (rented or mortgaged) without roommates, have your own vehicle for transportation, and live comfortably. These were worthy goals shared by both "yous," and this level of consumption is part of the plan.

Living on your own and within your means is your first "financial success" milestone.

In this first example, you are perceived as not having "made it" with the "American dream" until those around you perceive you as wealthy. According to our capitalist overlords, unless you are driving an expensive car (or cars), living in a costly home, going on vacations several times a year, and showing your "successful life" with pictures on social media, only then will people think you are wealthy!

But it doesn't make them like or dislike you anymore or any less.

News flash from my experience: They don't really care either way. They don't care about *your* wealth; they care about *their* wealth—you are just a comparison for them to "value" themselves against in our capitalist "utopia". Don't make the same mistake they and I did. Financial freedom is achieved through your dedication to building wealth and avoiding this "lifestyle" mirage that big businesses have spent hundreds of years promoting!

We will discuss this more throughout the book.

Corporations are spending billions to promote this idea of comparing our "wealth" to others in person and on social media. The vast majority of people you see (in life or on social media) are living this pseudo-wealthy lifestyle ON CREDIT! Some (many) actually have a low or even *negative* NAV.

Do you know what others don't see on those social media pages?

We don't see them (or this "American Dream" version of them) posting their monthly mortgage and car payments, credit card balances, or the amount spent on credit every month on this "wealthy lifestyle."

No, that is the dirty little secret about life in America (and in other capitalist societies).

Again, why am I using these quotations? As authors, we use quotations to demonstrate that something expressed in a word may not fully align with its intended meaning.

A lifestyle where you struggle to make payments on things you don't even truly own is a recipe for poverty, not wealth. For many, that is the "wealthy lifestyle".

Case in point—for most of us, including any person or persons in the above example, this level of perceived wealth is "bought" on credit. We don't really own anything that still has a loan payment, and we have to pay, with added interest, on all of those "lifestyle" credit cards.

This leads to my second example of the future you: an occasional and well-thought-out vacation, a car that is not as fancy (but still comfortable) but with lower payments or even paid off, a less expensive mortgage in a still lovely home, more money going into retirement accounts, and an ever-increasing NAV.

Your NAV!

This example is about you **actually** getting wealthier.

The other "you," if you follow the all-too-common "wealthy lifestyle" model, is getting poorer or at least not getting wealthier quickly. That is what corporations and capitalism want. They want you to spend on a lifestyle, one that is never enough. For example, if you get the base model of a Porsche, you then wish for the more expensive Turbo S version.

You should make your financial cuts by buying only things that bring you joy or save you discomfort, not to be fashionable or impress others.

During my life, I have lived in everything from a rented 140-square-foot (including the bathroom) apartment up to a mortgaged 4,000-square-foot home. Both extremes did the job. There is nothing wrong with wanting a nicer place, but think long and hard about what you want in that place. For me, the hassle of a house (I live in a condo now) was not worth the time or money. As an agent, I could not take care of a detached home. For many years, I spent more nights away than at home. For you, a detached home may be better.

Always think about what you want and what it costs.

My current condo is mortgaged and is a "good" debt. This just means that it is an appreciating asset that grows in value over time, unlike a depreciating asset such as a car. Getting into a mortgage or "buying" a home is an expensive endeavor that is increasingly becoming harder to achieve. Don't plan on that right away until you can both qualify for and afford that mortgage. It's even better to buy it in cash, but that takes even more time to achieve.

Constantly evaluate your spending and reevaluate regularly. Is it still worth it? If not, it goes.

Your car should be reliable, comfortable, dependable, and efficient (frugal in per-mile costs). Any vehicle that is not "just transportation" is paying more to impress or to be a joyful "toy". Keep that in mind when car shopping. If you are using your car a lot, comfort items may be worth it.

Also, if you can live somewhere (and want to) without needing a car at all—even better!

Unfortunately, America has been designed around the need for a car to get places. Some places can do without them, but those are few and usually more expensive. Overseas living is also a viable option to have a higher quality of life for less money, but you can achieve financial independence and stay in America if you wish. So, without further ado, let's get into the "Planning for Success" chapter and set you up for success!

Part One

The Basics

Chapter 1

Planning For Success

W e have all heard the term "failing to plan is planning to fail," and it is a truism.

Especially when (not if) Murphy decides to show up.

We learned about Murphy while I was in the US Army. He represents luck, usually bad luck.

Murphy's law is basically this: what can go wrong, will (at some point).

It is not to be pessimistic; it is to get soldiers to plan for eventualities. You won't always complete your mission with just the primary plan; in fact, you *rarely* do.

Do not despair.

The military also taught us some great acronyms for planning as officers that I am sharing now:

The opposite of "planning to fail" also has a truism— "planning to succeed." Just remember the Seven Ps for any successful endeavor:

"**Proper** prior planning prevents piss poor performance."

Everything important (and your financial life is **essential**) should have at least four plans built into its "proper prior planning." Remember this critical acronym —PACE.

Primary, Alternate, Contingency, and Emergency.

I will give an example from the PACE plan I made for my federal employment:

• Primary—6C Retirement. I did finish my 20 years to qualify for 6C (federal agent retirement program in FERS) and retire. I succeeded in this, but barely. They were pushing out older (and higher-paid) agents and using medical disqualification to do it. It often wasn't "for cause," as many of these agents had been working and succeeding in missions *as agents* for almost 20 years with these "disabilities". Almost all of our "legacy" agents (the ones nearing retirement eligibility) don't meet these medical standards (not surprising after 20 years of flying all hours of the day and night). Still, they didn't really push medical discharges until their largest contingent of agents was almost to retirement. Coincidence? I doubt it, but maybe. Always remember, it is great to get along with bosses and your co-workers and even like your job, but it can be taken away at any moment by your employer. They are not "family" and never will be.

• Alternate—Medical retirement. If I had been pushed into a medical retirement, this would have been my alternate. Medical retirement is hell. I watched agents who had been on medical retirement for years, still fighting to get or keep getting paid. Anyone who says they "got lucky" to go out on a medical retirement has never lived through this situation. I learned this directly from the agents going through it.

• Contingency—

First Contingency: FERS. Under this contingency plan, I am losing my 6C status and having to finish under regular FERS. This would have meant working five extra years, but I would only have received about 75% of what my 6C retirement would have been.

Second Contingency: Delayed retirement. After ten years of work with the federal government, you will be eligible to receive a delayed retirement. It will be small, and you can't collect without penalty until you are 62, with a 5% reduction each year you take it early. This is what would have happened if something went really wrong and I had to leave government service for any reason, such as a Reduction in Force. That is the government's version of a mass layoff.

• Emergency—I get fired from the government. This is the bad one. At that point, my delayed retirement would have to fall back under FERS (no 6C pension), and unless it is something really egregious, I would get my delayed retirement. Still, now I have to work at a much lower pay, until I qualify for both it and social security. I would be working (having to work) until my 60s—not the end of the world. I am working now as an author, but it is by my choice, not because of necessity.

So, always have at least four plans using this PACE system.

The good news about investing in general is this: You get to keep your investment accounts, no matter what!

Your 401 (k) and/or Roth IRA, along with whatever other wealth (and debts) you have accumulated, stay with you. So, as you can see, this plan cost me nothing to make, but gave me peace of mind about my options. If you work in the government, your PACE plan should look like this. If you don't, it still will be highly similar.

Any PACE plan will look like this:

P—The main (financial) goal goes as planned.

A—The less desirable secondary plan.

C—Undesirable result, but way better than nothing.

E—All goes to hell. But at least you leave with something more than when you started.

Things often do not go as planned. Planning is still essential—lots of planning and lots of plans—and being ready to make new ones. Murphy should only be a setback for the well-prepared, not the end of it all.

Chapter 2

Passive Income

S uppose you are like me (and you probably are); you have read a great many financial books. Almost all cover passive income, which simply means money you receive without having to work or do any labor for it.

Pensions, social security, ROI from investments, royalties, etc., are all forms of passive income.

This is the holy grail of financial independence.

Your 401(k), Roth IRA, and other financial investments will yield this return on investment (ROI). But how much? Well, if you get about 7% *long-term* (the approximate 200+ year historical real return on the S&P 500), then $100,000 would give you $7,000 a year. That's about $583 per month, before being taxed. Over the 220 years of research on the stock market (S&P 500 and equivalents), your money will be positive over any 17 years. Not the short run, but the long run. I extrapolated these numbers from a great book, *Stocks for the Long Run, Fifth Edition*, by Jeremy J. Siegel©.

Can you live on $7,000 a year? Probably not. But would that $583 gross income each month make your life better? Almost certainly. Sure, if it were a million instead, it would be enough.

Maybe.

Or maybe you need two million or ten? How do you know?

Because of your lifestyle.

If owning your own island and yacht is your yardstick for success, then plan to work—

Forever.

If you plan to be debt-free and own your home, particularly in a low-cost-of-living area, then perhaps a few hundred thousand dollars (or less), combined with just social security, will suffice.

It's your life and your choice.

No matter what you decide, your money will be in those accounts, accumulating and compounding year after year.

So, let us look at the phases of your life as we follow this plan. Do not be alarmed if you are "ahead" or "behind" the advice listed for the different "Life Phases." It could have been labeled in step order as well, just steps one through five. Feel free to think of it this way instead, if that helps you.

Alright! Let's get started!

Part Two

Stages of Life

Chapter 3

Youth

So, you are reading this as a young person. Congratulations! You have the most valuable resource of them all—

Time.

This is the thing that will make you the most money toward your financial independence.

But only if you spend it wisely.

The reason so many of us fail to achieve financial independence, or it takes longer than it needed to, is simple: we give in to capitalism. I am part of that group, I may add.

Yes, I achieved financial independence relatively young (at 51). But you can achieve it earlier or later. And again, it isn't a competition. Whether you are reading this at 15 or 65, the methodology is the same, and the goal is financial independence. It is not some nebulous thing; it is **your** financial independence we are going to achieve!

Where to start your journey, though?

As always, be pound-wise and penny-foolish.

Do you want a latte from Starbucks? Then go buy one!

Are you concerned you can't afford it? Then, it is time to look at the most crucial part of your life right now—your lifetime income.

Let's talk about my lifetime income to get started. Again, not to compare, but to learn from it—both good and bad. My story is only being shared with you so you can see how it *actually worked* over decades in this single example of one life lived toward this Financial Success goal:

I have always desired to be a protector; it is part of who I am. So, I became a soldier, then an armed security officer, then a police officer, and ended my career as a federal agent and instructor. That was my career and life. Most of you will not choose the same life path, and that is OK. Many do not know what they want in a career until later in life, or may change careers several times, and again, that is also OK!

But remember this—until you achieve financial independence, how much you are paid matters! Pay also includes benefits and other compensation. Your first job may not pay well, and that is fine. Mine didn't, either.

I didn't make a decent (high-earning) paycheck until I was in my thirties. It took me eight years to become a police officer and five more to become an agent. Then, it wasn't until my mid-forties that I saw six figures of income, and that was as a senior federal agent.

Guess where most of my 401(k) money came from?

It was a tie.

The amount my TSP investment increased from the smaller, earlier investments almost equaled the much more significant amounts I put in later. That is the beauty of compound interest, which we will discuss in more detail later. Later in the book, I will also focus on this concept in a real-world context.

So, get into a well-paying job—that is your goal in youth. Pick the field you want to be in and go after it! Do the things you need to do to get into the higher-paying positions in that field.

But, in the meantime, live your life. Have fun, but think about what gives you joy and balance the cost. As soon as you make enough to live (and not use credit to do it), start putting some money into your 401(k) with pre-tax dollars—even just one percent of your paycheck.

And don't ever stop until you are retired!

I heard all the same financial advice you did "growing up".

But, I can tell you now, after living for over half a century, the most essential piece of financial advice I was ever given—

Pay yourself first!

And don't take it out as an early withdrawal.

When I was young, the "future old man" that is me today seemed so far away. But here is something you should always consider: that money is yours! If you do this plan and five years from now, say "screw it" and pull it all out—who cares?

The ten percent penalty they charge you for early withdrawal will be significantly less than your accumulated return on investment (ROI), and it will have accrued pre-tax and tax-free.

This is a no-brainer!

So, don't think of it as money you've "thrown away" until you reach a more advanced age. If you manage this correctly, you can achieve financial independence in your 40s because you are starting early. If you accomplish this in your 30s, that's excellent! Even if it takes until your 50s, 60s, or later, that's still commendable. Remember, we are no longer comparing your worth to others, especially not based on material possessions.

Unfortunately, most Americans will never achieve financial freedom.

They will need to work to earn money until they die or live in poverty on Social Security benefits alone. If you achieve financial independence at *any* age, you will have done well!

One caveat for individuals with lower incomes is that, as long as you are in that low tax bracket, you may want to consider using after-tax dollars to fund a Roth IRA instead of pre-tax money, since you are paying little in taxes at the moment. I won't go into this in detail because our primary goal is to increase your income. The sad irony is, if you make a low enough income and thus qualify for a lower tax bracket, you probably don't have much money to invest right now anyway. If that is your situation, put that one percent of your paycheck (or more) into a *Roth* IRA instead until you are in a higher tax bracket.

Once your income rises—and it will—it will be more advantageous to use pre-tax dollars to invest instead. However, during the time you are in this situation, as I discussed with a brilliant young man, investing in a Roth IRA can be a good choice. Hopefully, you will soon be earning a higher paycheck, at which point pre-tax deductions will become more beneficial.

And what if you are older and living in this "poverty zone"? My advice (and examples) will still help.

Keep putting away a tiny amount (one percent of your income, at least) each month, and it will multiply over the years ahead. It is your money for your near future, "you". It's still a good habit to make, and there is no significant downside.

Do you have a safe and comfortable place to live and a lifestyle you can afford on your passive income (without having to work)? Then you are "successful" and financially independent.

You won!

Until then, you haven't "lost"; you are just working your way toward your goal. Just like with sports, if you are ahead and scoring more and more points (dollars), you are well on your way to winning.

Whether you want to live a lifestyle of reading, fishing, and hanging out with friends or travel the world on your personally owned 100-foot yacht, the definition of "Financial Success" for this book does not change.

Would you rather live a stress-free, enjoyable, but not expensive lifestyle? Or be on that yacht but constantly stressed about affording it? And worry about whether you will keep the income stream you need to afford it?

I would pass on the yacht.

If you would rather keep working and have that yacht, then kudos to you, but this book is probably not for you. Plus, if you can afford that, there is perhaps a silver spoon somewhere in your past. Even if you earned it all on your own (especially then), I would recommend lowering your lifestyle costs and "retiring" right now!

Remember, this book isn't about bashing the rich—you are not in this to compare yourself to others. This is about getting to the point where you don't need to work to earn money. You still can work and make money; that is OK. I am doing it right now. But now that I am retired and financially successful, I *choose* to share my life experiences through my writing, and I love that I can help others achieve success.

I also write other nonfiction and fiction books to spread knowledge or just to bring joy to others. This is fulfilling for me, and it is only possible because of the decisions I made (good and bad) over a thirty-plus-year career.

That is where you will be—and starting young, probably even sooner than I did.

There will never be a time you look back and say, "I wish I had saved less and spent more." Still, do all the activities and life goals you want, but just be intelligent about it and pay yourself first. Take that pre-tax money, throw it in the S&P 500, and forget about it until you retire early.

You don't have to learn about investing in individual stocks (or anything else) unless you want to. But that investing is always done with the money "leftover" after paying your Individual Retirement Accounts (IRAs). For me, that amount of money didn't happen until my late 40s. Only then did I max out both my 401(k) and Roth. That being said, if I had followed this advice when I was younger, I would have been a multi-millionaire today!

Please, learn from me and achieve more success—and sooner.

It isn't about a specific amount of money, either. It is about a financial situation, a lifestyle where you don't *need* to work to be comfortable. That is the "amount" of money you are striving to achieve.

The amount that achieves your Financial Success.

Chapter 4

Young Adult

Alright, you are now in the full-time workforce. Congrats!

Maybe you are in your teens with your first summer job, or you are in your 20s. I have news for you: if you are working for a wage, even as a child, the "young adult" section applies to you.

So does the respect of being called "Sir" or "Ma'am." If you are old enough to work, you are old enough to be respected for doing so!

Unless you have some seriously high-level connections, your first jobs are not going to be huge money-makers. Your first financial goal is getting into a higher-paying job in your chosen career. It may take advanced training and/or college degrees before you can get into that career. It will also probably take years of experience, after all that, before you get your first "high-paying" job. That is OK; it is actually atypical if it doesn't take years. The

19

sooner you get there, though, the sooner you can work toward your end goal—financial independence.

Your goals at this stage are threefold:

1) Get paid more than your lifestyle costs and keep your cost of living down.

2) Start investing in pre-tax retirement accounts.

Obviously, both will be easier to accomplish the more you earn and the cheaper your lifestyle.

Be smart.

It is OK to have roommates or to live at home with your parents if you are still not making a lot—it won't be forever. So, I want to add a third goal that helps with the first two and is enormous in helping you become and stay debt-free—

3) Limit/avoid debt.

Some debt may be necessary to obtain the training or degrees needed for good pay (or even entry into) your chosen field. That's acceptable, but try to limit it as much as possible. Corporate greed wants the miracle of compound interest to work for their profit, and they achieve this through the interest *you* pay on your debts. Our goal is to do the opposite: maintain no debts and allow *you* to benefit from compound interest on *your* investments. If you already have debt (most people do), your goal is to put at least one percent, or your full company-match amount, into retirement accounts pre-tax with every paycheck. If your company does not offer it, just do it with a brokerage firm.

(You should open a brokerage account, such as Fidelity© or Charles Schwab©, because you will need it for your Roth IRA down the road anyway. Plus, it is more "portable" when you switch jobs in the private sector.)

This one percent does not sound like much because it isn't—you won't even notice it. But that money will compound the principal and the Return on Investment (ROI) many times over, for *decades*. Do not skip this!

Use the rest of your discretionary extra income to pay off debts, especially high-interest credit cards.

Yes, reduce your lifestyle costs now and only allow "lifestyle creep" to occur as you make more money. But even then, take a hard look at how you can keep those costs down. Don't "go up" in what you spend each month just because you make more money! Sure, give yourself some kind of reward for that achievement, but don't get on the American bandwagon of "keeping up with the Joneses".

Also, advance your career and pay down that debt, especially as you start to earn more money.

Another note on careers: You do not need to make six figures to achieve financial independence, but the more passive income you accumulate and the less debt (eventually, it should be zero), the better! For that reason, a higher income *is* needed.

You and I have been there when it comes to erroneous financial advice.

All the BS over "cutting out lattes" to make a small income work is terrible advice—it will only deliver a tiny amount of return. If that is what you need to do to afford the one percent for now, then OK, cut back some.

On that note, I have an automatic espresso machine, and I use it several times a day. It cost me $500, and I have made *thousands* of cups of coffee and espresso with it. So, it really has paid for itself. (It is a Delonghi Magnifica© automatic espresso machine. I get no monetary or other compensation from them, but this machine is the most durable thing I have ever purchased.)

But I still buy the occasional $5+ latte—and I plan to continue.

I also buy avocado toast at restaurants.

Limiting and eliminating debt, investing in a 401(k)/Roth, keeping your lifestyle costs down, earning a higher income, increasing your retirement contributions, and not drawing from those retirement accounts—this is what will make you financially independent or even wealthy.

Skipping all your lattes won't.

To sum up, work hard to get into that higher-paying career, and don't worry that it takes years—that is normal. Keep your debts down and start investing one percent of each paycheck, or more, as soon as you are employed.

That's it.

After doing this, see where you are when you get to the next chapter of your life.

Chapter 5

Career Adult

The next chapter of your life—the career adult.

So, you are further along in your career now, in the position you worked so hard to get, and starting to earn a higher income. That's sweet!

Now what?

The underlying principles from the earlier chapters still apply (and always will until you achieve financial freedom).

Now, we are upping your game!

You are approaching the point in life where your "lifestyle" costs have crept up. These include having your own place, car, and essential luxuries (like an espresso machine). These increases in lifestyle costs are reasonable.

Here is what you don't want: an expensive car, expensive hobbies, or lots of useless "stuff."

Remember intellectual minimalism!

Intellectual minimalism is based on the concept of intellectual hedonism.

Intellectual hedonism means living for what brings you happiness and joy now *and in the future.*

An example is enjoying experiences in your life now, but also saving for the future.

An example of hedonism is your dog. If you give it a giant steak dinner with all the trimmings, it will gobble up every bite and then get sick to its stomach—and it will do this every night.

People are just the same as any other animal. If we do whatever we want now, without concern for future pain, that is hedonism. If we do what we wish to, but factor in future costs, that is intellectual hedonism.

If we throw everything out that we don't absolutely need, that is minimalism (this is for my example only; I hope not to anger minimalists with this genuinely overly-concise version). However, if we only buy and keep what we truly use regularly and value, and part with the rest, *that* is intellectual minimalism.

I didn't practice intellectual minimalism well until recently. The number of things people buy, get rid of, never use, rebuy, etc., is staggering. Most Americans waste thousands of dollars every year.

Use this money to invest instead of buying "things".

If you want to set aside money for an item that you *really* want and will *really* use, go for it, but if you haven't used something in a year, get rid of it. Sell it, donate it, gift it, or just throw it away; only keep what brings you actual value and joy.

Minimalism becomes more difficult the more you set a "new normal" for your lifestyle. You can live a very comfortable life without expensive things or trying to "live rich". Warren Buffett is a good role model for this. He had the same house and car for many years, both relatively modest for a millionaire, much less a billionaire!

Again, do not be discouraged by "losing" your money to retirement investments. As you make more income, you can enjoy the good lifestyle that you have created without having to spend a lot more. Every raise can yield an inexpensive "reward"—followed by increasing your investments. Plus, the older we get, the closer to retirement we get. All that money is YOUR MONEY. You can collect it anytime you *want*, but you won't because you don't *need* it.

Feel free to skip ahead in the book at any time to learn how to get the most expensive "optional" things in life (children, homes, etc.).

I want to cover something else that is critically important—regret.

The most immense pain you will feel (besides the loss of loved ones) is **regret**. Live your life well, do the things that really matter to you, but always think about the trade-offs in life, including to your wealth. If having kids will delay your retirement (it will), that is OK. But realize it will and be OK with that. If not, don't have them!

Same with anything else. The more expensive it is, the more you need to consider how to go about it or whether you want just to skip that expense entirely. This book is about being smart with your money to achieve your best life, not about scrounging every penny and being a miser until you become a millionaire! If that is your thing, there are plenty of other books in that vein.

To sum up, you should follow the same principles as

before, but at this point in your life, your retirement investments should be north of 10% of your total gross income,
and your debts should be heavily reduced or eliminated. If
not, no worries. Follow the advice and pay them off.
People (including me) have failed at this because we get
out of debt and then choose to go right back into debt, just
to get *things*.

Stay focused and disciplined, and it will pay off
for you.

That, I DO promise!

Chapter 6

Late Career

O K, we are finally at "a certain age".

The young version of us would be amazed as we have progressed to middle age and are well into the best-paying years of our careers. For many, this is when they START thinking about retirement!

You, however, are already well on your way.

If you have a mortgaged home, you are on your way to paying it off. If you have kids, they are almost grown (and their college and retirement are already well funded—see the "Pre-birth" chapter for why you were already set for this). Also, you have accumulated a pretty nice nest egg for retirement.

Oh, wait, you haven't done all of this?

Guess what, most of us haven't either, that is why I wrote this book!

Whether you started this plan at 15 or 65, the process is the same—you will have less debt, more money, and better passive income every year you do this. So, every year and every month will make you better off than before, even if you then "quit" the program. (Please don't; it is your money, not mine or anyone else's.)

This is a straightforward process to master, but it is tough to stay disciplined enough to do it! The longer you do it, though, the easier it will get.

A little anecdote on that...

I look back at the times when I reduced the amount of money I contributed to my 401(k) and investments, and—every time—it was because I "needed" more money for something I didn't really need: an expensive car, or to pay off debts for things I had already bought (but didn't need), or to maintain a lifestyle that was far beyond what I needed to feel comfortable and happy. Get off the "things" bandwagon— NOW!

As you hit your maximum contribution limits with your higher income, you can start adding the "matching funds" that the IRS lets you have the year you turn 50 or older. We are going to max these also. If you are maxing out your 401(k) and Roth, you need nothing else to achieve that financial freedom (besides staying out of debt). If you want to do more, great, but this amount will give you everything you need and then some.

This plan will get you to your financial freedom: how fast is up to you, but it will happen.

If I had had the will and determination then, to follow through on what I am writing about right now, I would be a multi-millionaire today. That is a mathematical fact.

So, I want to help *you* achieve financial success.

Hearing from you about your success would make my day! The idea that I helped you down the path to financial freedom means that this book has meaning and that I helped another human to have a better life. That is my biggest reward by far! I know it sounds cheesy, and you may call out "BS" on this statement, but I genuinely mean it. I have read so many books and tried to follow this advice when I was poor in my twenties. If I had followed through on even most of the advice I learned then, I would have achieved my financial success *much* sooner.

I want that success for you.

We have never met, but knowing I helped you—even just a little—to have a better life is important to me. I was an instructor for many years and, now that I think about it, decades. I love teaching, as it allows me to impart knowledge. Knowledge is built on the innumerable years of research and experience by others. You don't have to learn concepts from the ground up. Use what others have to teach and be a master of your trade: the trade of building your wealth and financial freedom.

All books are compilations of knowledge from millions of others, added to by the authors. What I am teaching is a well-established guideline for your success. We don't make it alone; we all need help. Collaborate and always keep learning.

Let's continue the journey to make you financially successful.

Chapter 7

Retirement

CONGRATULATIONS!
You did it! You are financially successful!
By our definition, it means this—
Your passive income (without earning a wage working for others) covers your lifestyle without *having* to work. You have no debts (with the possible exception of a first mortgage). You no longer have to work or worry about money.

That was our measurement of ultimate success.

It is my sincere hope that my book helped you achieve this. Being financially independent is one of the most wonderful things in the world. Now, you can plan vacations, visit and spend time with friends and family, enjoy leisure activities... or just choose to do nothing at all.

The best part is that you can find fulfillment by doing the things that bring you joy and, yes, even things that make you feel like you are a contributing member of your world, and helping others. For me, that is the joy of writing books—I want to educate and entertain others with my writing.

What do *you* want?

Now you can decide. Surprisingly, you will discover new things that give your life meaning as you start your financially successful retirement. You can choose if there is another job or career you want to try. You can choose if there is a pastime you like; it can even be something that makes money for you. The best part is that you *decide* what you wish to do, even if it is just never to work again. (By the way, I tried that; you may be surprised to find that just "doing nothing" doesn't seem to work for you... at least it didn't for me.)

At this point, you continue to pay down and pay off what little debt (if any) you have. Hopefully, that is just a first mortgage or no debt at all, and your passive income covers that regardless. Just don't make new debts, and you are forever free from *having* to work.

Now is the time when you start asking yourself a simple question—

"If I have enough passive income, and I am accumulating wealth every month and year, where does it go when I die?"

In the next part of this book, Pitfalls and Planning, there is a chapter, Afterlife, that covers your legacy—where your money and assets will go after you die.

Part Three

Pitfalls and Planning

Chapter 8

The Big Three

Pitfalls.

We all fall into them; the goal is to limit them, especially the BIG ones!

The best way to make money is to find a life partner who shares your goals and then help each other achieve them. The problem with that? Not to be morbid, but the vast majority of relationships, including marriages, fail. Which leads to our first big financial mistake, which we will cover more below—

Divorce.

Sure, you can be a "sugar baby" and make money through a divorce. But this is not a guide on how to get rich by immorally taking it from others. That said, if it is *genuinely* a "mutually beneficial" relationship, then go for it.

However, it should include a pre-nuptial that you both agree to enthusiastically.

Getting rich, for the ordinary person, is not a zero-sum

game. You do not have to harm someone else to enrich yourself.

So, let's discuss the enormous wealth destroyers that can upend your financial plans (and cause a lot of other pain, too).

These three are the biggest:

1) Divorce. This is a biggie! My advice? Do not get married.

But, as with all important life events, if you do, plan it!

Get a pre- and post-nuptial agreement and sign them! This is not romantic, but so what? Neither is marriage. Hear me out before saying, "WTF ..."

The *custom* of marriage is based on religion. The *LAW* on marriage is a terrible union of two parties into one legal entity. Marriage is a legal contract and should be looked at that way. No two corporations would ever merge by signing the legal documents of marriage—that should tell you something.

So why do it at all?

It's simple: the government in the United States wants you to be married. They give you tax breaks, health insurance requires it in order to share a "plus one" on your plan, and even car insurance can be affected. It makes your assets (and debts) common "property" that you both are responsible for.

On the good side, if you both are on the same page, it does help with sharing some costs (especially a mortgage).

However, divorce is not just possible but statistically likely. Sorry to be a buzz-kill, but the time to talk about and sign legal documents (that will come up in your divorce proceedings) is *before* your marriage, not after. Sign these documents, mainly because you *do* love your spouse.

If you don't need or want to get married, then don't. How much you love someone isn't determined by a document issued by the state.

2) Children. This is probably the most significant financial cost in your life. To save the most, don't have them, but if you are going to, plan it! (Are you sensing a recurring theme?)

Having a child will not "save" your relationship. It adds enormous stress and cost to your life. Suppose it is what you both want, though, then that is OK. Just realize the costs. We have already gone into the actions to take *before* having your first child and will do so more in Chapter 12, *Pre-Birth*. If you want to avoid future custody issues, then sole-parent adoption (while you are single and not in a serious relationship) is also an option. If I owned a dog, I would resolve any future custody issues with my partner before ever buying it. Needless to say, you should do that before having a child! There is a lot of love between you and your spouse, and there will be with your future kids as well. Financial planning, even for the possibility of a divorce, shows you **do** care, not that you don't.

3) Medical. As the only economically developed country with the dubious honor of not having some kind of

universal healthcare, this is also a pitfall. Other developed countries (the other 32 out of 33 OECD countries) all have this. Their citizens don't have "pre-existing" conditions that allow insurers not to cover—or grotesquely inflate—their medical costs. So we have to get it as a "benefit" through (usually full-time) employment in a company or government job.

Only in America.

In the other OECD countries, their citizens don't go bankrupt from common serious illnesses or injuries, ones that can happen to any of us at any time.

For this reason, you *must* obtain good health care coverage in the United States. Even then, unforeseen medical issues can derail your ability to achieve financial freedom and wealth. So, get medical coverage for at least the significant costs.

You will hear people saying, "We don't need universal *socialist* health care in America!"

And *we* don't (I have FEHB health insurance as a federal retiree)—but *you* do!

This book isn't about politics; it's about finances. And our medical system in America can ruin you financially in a heartbeat. You *must* obtain it or obtain foreign medical coverage as an expat. If you don't have coverage and get seriously sick or injured, you and your family have a high chance of becoming bankrupt.

Chapter 9

Financial "Experts"

One of the biggest things I learned was about avoiding financial "experts".

Don't get me wrong, paying for a good accountant for your taxes and an estate planner for your durable medical and financial power of attorney and will are still great ideas. Just don't pay for any financial advice on a "percentage basis". If you do choose to use a financial planner (I did not; I just read A LOT about finances), only pay them set fees for specific services. Over 80% of professional hedge fund managers underperform the S&P 500 over ten years.

Think about that.

These "professionals" underperform the most common (and easiest) benchmark to achieve.

Don't pay them to lose money for you.

Just max (as much as you can) your 401(k) with pre-tax money and put it in that benchmark (the S&P 500).

Especially as you make more gross income, all the money you would have paid in tax adds to what you can put in.

Already maxed? Congratulations again!

Less than 20% of wage earners achieve this milestone!

Now, max your Roth IRA with after-tax money in a brokerage firm, also. This money grows tax-free and is collected tax-free! And, in hard times (only if you absolutely must), you can withdraw your investment amounts without penalty—not the earnings, though.

Currently, you can invest over $30,000 a year this way—$23,500 in your 401(k) pre-tax and $7,000 after-tax into your Roth IRA.

That number goes up to almost $40,000 if you are turning 50 or older this year—$31,00 with "catch-up contributions" into your 401 (k) and $8,000 into your Roth IRA.

Additionally, a new provision allows individuals aged 60 to 63 to contribute an extra $11,250 (instead of $7,500) as a catch-up contribution to their 401(k), which brings the total maximum personal contributions to $34,750 per year.

Your employer contributions (if you are fortunate enough to have them) can also be added to your 401(k)—up to a total of $70,000 each year. This contribution limit increases to $77,500 for those turning 50 this year (or older), and $81,250 annually for those aged 60-63!

OK, OK, I know what you are saying—

"Must be nice."

This high level of investment is the end goal, not the starting one. I didn't max out my retirement contributions until later in my career, but the 5-10% I put in year after year before that really added up!

This is the take-home message I want you to receive: Your biggest regrets will be the things in life you could have done better but didn't, or the things you wanted to do or be but didn't.

You can never change the past.

PUT MONEY INTO YOUR RETIREMENT ACCOUNTS EVERY PAYCHECK!

I cannot stress this enough. If you do everything else wrong and retire with no other assets, this money is there for you. This money, combined with any passive income (and any owned assets), will give you that financial independence. Even if you stay out of debt and do everything else right, unless you have a high passive income, you will need this money.

Learn from experiences, both the good and the bad, and apply those lessons to your current and future decisions. The more you can learn from—and act on—the mistakes and successes of others, the more successful you will be, and the sooner you will achieve financial success!

Chapter 10

The Market

Ah, yes, the "Market."

We hear about it every day. Whether it's the DOW or the S&P 500, it represents the largest companies in the world. By owning shares of the S&P 500, you also own the DOW Jones Industrial Average (the top 30 stocks by market value). The S&P 500, as the name suggests, includes approximately 500 of the largest companies in America, many of which are also the largest in the world. The last time I looked, it was actually 505 companies. Therefore, it's a safe bet that the top 500 companies *in the world* will perform well during your lifetime, just as they have in mine and for ten generations before.

Again, there are no guarantees.

However, you need to invest your money; there's no other option. If you simply hoard it—whether under your mattress or in a low-yield savings account—you will lose money over time. Remember that pesky inflation? That's the devaluing of the dollar each year. That is the increase in what goods and services cost. Do you know who provides those inflated goods and services? Companies.

So, the best hedge against inflation and to produce exponential profit for your investment over time is to put it in a diverse mix of the largest and safest companies in the S&P 500. We have already discussed what you should do to "play the market" and invest.

Maximize your 401(k) (or at least the employer match —ALWAYS do this amount) and, after that, contribute to your Roth IRA.

Already did? Fantastic, you are done!

No, really, you are done.

Just keep doing that, and in a couple of decades, you will never have to work for money again. But if you also want to learn about individual stocks and investments, go for it, but avoid leverage at all costs. Leverage is using debt, such as margin (debt provided by brokerage companies) or credit cards, for capital. If you are not using leverage, the max you can lose is just the money you put in. I will not cover which ones to buy or why in this book. However, I will cover one thing I learned well from others:

The best holding period is forever.

I looked back on my life and that of a much wealthier sibling and noticed something true for us both: we would have been wealthier just keeping the stocks we bought. Instead of buying and selling, timing the market, hedging, and all the other "professional investor" tricks we had learned, we would have made more money by passively investing in the S&P 500.

And the individual stocks I did buy? If I had just "held them," I would have made more than all of the trading I did over the years.

From 2016 to 2021, I made a significant amount of money off meme stocks (a.k.a. micro stocks and speculative trading), but I also lost money by holding on to some of them. It turns out that the time to sell meme stocks was in the first quarter of 2021. I sold many, but not all, and watched the ones left plummet in value.

In the end?

You guessed it. Just buying and holding, or better yet, just putting it in the S&P 500, would have made me more in the long run.

Live and learn. Or, in your case, read and learn (much cheaper).

So, we need to delineate between "investing" and "speculating". If you are concerned about not holding a stock for over a year (to take advantage of long-term capital gains) because you are concerned the niche it is in may "boom and bust," it is not an investment.

You are gambling or speculating.

Not a bad thing, just know that you are.

I invested in Tesla stock (stock ticker: TSLA) from 2018 to 2020. I "wisely" sold my stock, which I had purchased at $200 a share, for $800 a share. This was a brilliant move!

Sadly, for me, it went up after that, split several times, and was effectively at over $6,000 a share only a year later. However, it could have just as easily been Enron or Pets.com stock (both still worth zero). According to Tesla's shareholder reports, they almost went bankrupt more than once during that time.

Individual stocks, well-researched and with good fundamentals, are investments. But index funds, which are *lots* of stocks, are a much safer bet for your long-term wealth.

Chapter 11

Afterlife

Estate Planning

We all are going to die, sooner or later.

We only live once and then leave behind whatever actions we took for decades, good and bad alike.

Your debts will die with you, but they will be collected from your estate before the remainder is paid to your beneficiaries (with the exception of life insurance and IRA payouts). If you are married, the two of you are a single legal entity, so your partner will inherit those debts. (Technically, they are your debts as a married couple.) Your assets will also be passed down. How?

Suppose you plan in advance, which you should: Your estate would be managed through a legally binding will or trust that you establish with an estate planner. Or, if you are married, many items of your estate will automatically go to your spouse. Either way, still set one up.

Why did you set it up this way? Because you learned from my example. I had a serious eye-opener about our legal system in America. What got me to see an estate planner? It was a learning experience from someone else, just like what you are reading about me now.

When my father died, he died without a legally enforceable will. He did not have many assets, but he and his multi-decade live-in girlfriend lived in Arizona. She didn't marry him because of her Social Security, and she wanted to have separate finances—no problems with that.

But when he died, that all changed.

My brother managed my late father's estate affairs after he died, and I am grateful that he did. He had to hire a lawyer to file an injunction just to keep my father's "non-wife" from being evicted from their trailer in a 55+ community (only 72 hours after his death). Why? Because they were not legally married and had not set up a deed transfer.

Sounds complicated, doesn't it? It was.

If they had spent about $200 on a deed transfer, it would have saved her significant stress and avoided a lengthy, costly legal proceeding.

So here is the thing I learned from that: If you couldn't care less about the headaches, trials, and tribulations your heirs will go through (even if you don't have many assets or wealth), then skip this chapter.

But if you actually *like* or *love* your heirs, you need to plan appropriately!

It cost me something like $2,000 to set up my entire estate plan. It was expensive and worth every penny. Not only did it give me an enforceable will, but it also gave me a durable power of attorney, **enforceable** medical directives, and assumable deeds for durable goods and real estate, such as my car and condo. Without those things, your estate is in the hands of probate (even with a will) and your doctor's choices on care (not yours) if you are not able to communicate. Not where you want you or your heirs to be!

I know this for a fact after watching the hell my brother went through to help my father's "widow" from being evicted. If you are "living in sin" and not legally married (like me), you have even more work to do to protect those you love. Do not leave their fate to chance!

If you are early in life, still set it up when you can—but soon.

If you are later in life, especially if others are dependent on your assets or income, then you must do this ASAP!

* * *

Life Insurance

This is a tough one.

First, if you are single and no one you care about *needs* financial assistance from you, then don't get it. Actuaries determine your payments, along with those of others, and then choose the amount you will pay for a certain level of coverage. They are for-profit companies, not altruists. They are betting, quite accurately, that you will probably not collect more than the premiums you pay them.

So, only do this if you *must* provide money, such as for

children or a minimum quality of life for a non-working spouse. You don't need life insurance if your assets or residual (post-death) income/wealth are sufficient. If not, you should have *some* life insurance.

That's the catch.

If you already have wealth, such as retirement accounts, you don't need the ongoing expense. And if you don't, you have to pay to get it, which then slows your ability to become wealthy. My recommendation is to set yourself (and your partner) up so that you don't need it at all. If you have (or are planning to have) children, your estate also needs to address the two most significant costs in your children's lives—college and retirement. Those should be partially or fully covered by the trust (or 529 plans) you have already set up. You only need enough life insurance to cover bills until your partner is on his or her feet and taking your place as the breadwinner and head of household. The bulk of their inheritance money should be your accumulated wealth, but you must prepare for an untimely (early) death.

Unless you need to provide a certain minimum (and it should be the minimum), I would put every penny of what you would have spent on premiums into your retirement account instead. Also, remember if you are paying $150 a month in premiums, and let's say you are in an effective tax rate of 25%, then you can put $200 a month *pre-tax* into your retirement account. That will add up to *a lot* of money over time. And that money can go to whoever you would have given the life insurance to.

Gifts

As I write this (in 2025), the IRS limit for lifetime gifts without paying tax is $13,999,000 for a single filer (or $27,980,000 for married couples).

So, do you think the US is all about the rich yet? If you do, what gave it away?

Unless you are part of the 0.1% of the US population to whom going over the exemption applies, this is not your problem. There are no tax consequences to giving your money away.

None.

Once you are well enough off, feel free to give things and money away while alive or after you die. On that note, let's talk about the annual exclusion for gifts.

There are a lot of misconceptions about this.

As of 2025, the limit is $19,000 per recipient per year ($38,000 if you are married). This is the maximum yearly amount you can give without having to count it toward your lifetime exemption (of 14/28 million dollars). So, if you bought into the capitalist elite's BS about estate taxes being about you, think again!

This is just the amount per year that can be given tax-free *in addition* to the exemption limit.

If this taxation is an issue for you, you may have accidentally bought the wrong book! But no worries—it costs you less than .00002% of your net worth...

And congratulations, you are definitely financially independent!

The only "consequence" for us 99.9% is having to report it to the IRS if we give more than $19,000 per year per recipient—no tax is paid on the overage; it just counts toward the $14 million limit. We can only hope (fantasize?) to exceed the tens of millions of dollars to *start* paying taxes on it...

Anyone asking where we would get the money for our "welfare" programs, like universal healthcare that every other developed country has for its citizens, should consider cutting this exemption to a measly million or two, or at least cut it back in half (to only 7/14 million) where it used to be.

Chapter 12

Pre-Birth

So you decided to have children.

Congratulations!

You have done the one thing that "costs" the most. That said, it isn't a mistake. It will be expensive, to be sure, but if that is what you want in your life, you should do it. Remember the immense anguish you will have when you are done with your career and peak earning years if you don't.

Regret is a real thing—ask anyone older than yourself.

Far more important than anything else, even financial independence, is doing the things that matter most to you. If your dream is to have a child or be a doctor, or whatever else, you better do it, or at least have given it your best shot! You will only have one life. If you don't do the most essential things in life *for yourself*, regret will stalk you in your later years, when it is too late to do anything about it.

"Wait a minute! You said having children was the costliest financial "mistake" I could make!"

Yes, I did say that, and if it *is a mistake*, it is! However, if having children is essential to you, you should do it. Even if it *was* unplanned, you will still find great joy in being a parent. Just like any major expense, though, you need to *plan* for it.

I do not have kids; they were not a priority in my life, but I have been in live-in relationships with women who have. I learned from them, just as I hope you can learn from my five decades of life experiences, both the good *and* the bad of my life. Always look around at others, not to compare yourself against, but to see what they did well and what they did not.

I cannot pretend to tell you everything you need to know about raising children, but I will cover the most important *financial* things to do. As always, I am assuming you will follow the advice of having health insurance and a small emergency reserve of cash. Beyond that, your child will need money, especially for retirement and college. Do you want your child never to have to worry about retirement? How about college?

You do?

Start planning now, then. And I mean *right* now—even if it is before you have that child.

Estate planners can help you set up a trust for your child and your potential grandchildren as well. The next step will be to fund it through your brokerage firm.

Visit your brokerage firm (you already have a brokerage account, right?) and establish the accounts after creating the trust with your estate planner. At this time, you should hire an estate planner and a reputable generational wealth CPA.

Now, go start funding it.

The amount is going to sting. If you are going to be (or are) pregnant, then you are probably not in the late stages of your career, but hopefully, you are making good money and in a good financial position. If not, you need to get there, and fast! Children are going to make things **a lot** harder. They require a lot of money, time, and *energy*.

So, let's get their trusts done and at least partially funded *before* they are born.

I watched a co-worker who maxed out his 401(k) (in the federal government, it is the Thrift Savings Program, or TSP) from his first day and never took a withdrawal. He did not leave it all in the S&P 500 (if he had, it would have been about double according to his math), but even in conservative accounts, his TSP was almost worth a million dollars. He was forty-five at the time. He had been faithfully depositing the maximum contribution since he started with the Feds at twenty-two.

I only had half of that amount because I made withdrawals, didn't max it the whole time, and did "time the market" a couple of times. Luckily, I broke even on market timing, but I missed gains (and it was dumb—FYI). However, my ROI during that time was still better than his, although mine was a little less than the S&P 500's performance.

Here is the amazing thing: if either of us had a thousand dollars in that account when we were born, we would have about $64,000 for each thousand at 60 (based on real-world S&P 500 performance over the last 200 years). Now, imagine that thousand sitting for a *hundred* years and going to *his* children's retirement. If his parents had put about \$15,625 in at his birth, he would retire at 60 with a million. But, if they put in only a thousand for *his* children, it would be about a million also (assuming he has kids at 35 and they collect at 65). As long as it didn't exceed the \$14 million estate exemption, it would only be taxed on the amount it gained each year. Yes, tax law can change dramatically over a hundred years, I know.

"But that is so far away; why would I do that?"

Because the effects are immediate. If you want it to be a secret to motivate success in your progeny, go ahead. But if you let it be known, you will get immediate gratification **and** delayed gratification. The recipients (your children) will have an enormous load taken off their shoulders, as will their future children. You must remember that a million dollars for your child's children not only removes much of the burden of saving for retirement for them, but it also saves the burden of saving for your grandchild's retirement for *your* child.

Add in a tax-deferred 529 plan (for college) for your unborn child, and you have their education paid for, also for a few thousand dollars, as a one-time payment.

Generational wealth is powerful. And if you "skip a generation" with some of that money, it becomes *exponentially* larger.

This information came from a conversation about it with my estate planner. It is also called a perpetuity trust. So, of course, there is something called "rules against perpetuities" to keep you from using this tactic forever. However, each state has a maximum timeframe the trust can exist. It may vary by state; however, in Colorado, the limit is one thousand years. If you are not personally paying the tax, the trust can generally be administered by the trust manager for around one or one-and-a-half percent per year. Add in paying tax each year on the earnings, and it will reduce the earnings to maybe only 5 or 6 percent for the S&P 500 (or its equivalent) over time. And remember, the most significant gains for that are over time.

I don't care if you start with only $100; you can add more later (but the sooner, the better!).

Once that trust is done, compound interest will replace decades of investing from a single small amount now. I wish I had done this earlier, and I will be setting one up in the next few years. It will be fun to think of what $1,000 compounded over a century (or centuries) would become!

Let's look more at intergenerational wealth accumulation in the next chapter.

Chapter 13

Generational Skipping

G enerational wealth.

No chapter is needed to explain how the rich keep getting richer in America—it's called intergenerational wealth.

Do you have less than 14 million dollars in assets to leave to your next of kin? No worries; you will pay ZERO tax on that! Welcome to America—the land of "Hurray for the ultra-rich and to hell with everyone else." However, one "trickle-down" effect is that anyone can use many of their (ultra-rich people's) tools as well. The big secret is that most people don't want to (or can't) spend the time, effort, and money to use these tools. Once set up, though, they are typically quite hands-off.

So, this chapter is more about leaving money for future generations, using what is called "generational skipping"— for those who are not decamillionaires already.

When I worked for the federal government, they had a program called the Combined Federal Campaign (for making charitable donations through paycheck deductions). If you contribute to charitable organizations from your paycheck, especially if you claim a tax deduction for it, good for you! You are doing a wonderful thing.

However, if you want to maximize your contribution (to any cause, including your heirs), consider the concept of "generational skipping."

So, what is this thing that I speak of?

It is simple. When I looked at how much money is wasted by many NPOs (non-profit organizations)—it is enormous! Much of your money is not used for your end goal but instead goes to administrative and other, frankly, BS expenses. So, let's "skip the middleman".

If you have enough to leave a sizable amount, then set up that perpetual trust we talked about.

You put your money into a long-term investment (like the S&P 500), and then you tell that trust when, how much, and to whom it goes, along with specific instructions on how and where that money will be spent. This is much more efficient!

Let's use an example:

Say you love animals and want to contribute to the SPCA© charity. It is OK to do that, but let's look at the math. You donate twelve thousand dollars. I don't know the exact overhead, but let's be kind and assume half does not go straight to the needed animals but instead is "wasted" on other non-related overhead for the organization. So, you "net" $6,000 directly to the animals. You did well.

Now, let's assume you spend that $12,000 putting it into an irrevocable trust instead. Maybe $2,000 goes into making the trust, and $10,000 is invested in a low-expense S&P 500 inside the trust—or just given directly. Already, more goes to those animals in need. You did even better.

But what if we wait?

For our model, we will use the historical real return of the market at approximately 7%, which is its real return over 220+ years (nominal amount minus inflation is a real return). One of the books I read, *Stocks for the Long Run*, by Jeremy J. Siegel©, showed approximately a 6.8% real return. For this example, we are assuming 7.2%—just for the ease of my model and not melting our brains with math. Every ten years, at that rate, it will double. Then the next ten years, that new amount will be doubled again.

Exponentially.

Now, let's set your trust for 100 years before the funds begin to be dispersed, allowing it to increase by over 1,000 times. So, that 10,000 dollars? It is now worth $10 million. Maybe in 100 years, humanity will all get along, and we won't have strays anymore. I doubt that. So, would you rather invest $10,000 at your death and get $5,000 of value, or wait a century and have it be 10 million?

I know which I would pick.

After all, if you are dead, you won't notice the difference in time. Or, if you are right about religion, your immortal soul won't be in a rush and will love seeing what ten million dollars can do. Win, win.

What about if you are less altruistic? How about giving it to your grandkids instead?

Let's say you are having your first child. At birth, you gift your child one thousand dollars in an irrevocable trust —except you disperse it to his or her children instead.

Now, they will never need to worry about retirement, nor will their parents have to set aside money for it. Why? Because they will have over a million dollars to give to their child or children. A real million dollars, too, as it will be equivalent to today's dollars plus inflation. Yes, some taxes may apply, such as the generation-skipping transfer (GST) tax, which is levied in addition to estate and gift taxes (which are effectively zero tax). But it is still a million dollars before tax! Oh, and the current limit on the GST exemption? You guessed it—the same 13.99 million dollars per individual (double that if married).

But what if they don't have kids? Easy, add a directive for the executor of the estate to disperse those funds differently at a certain age. Such as "If my child does not have children by age fifty, all proceeds go to them directly instead." Simple.

How do you do this?

You leave $1,000 in an irrevocable trust for their children to retire on. Let's assume your child has children at 35 and their child retires at 65—that thousand? It will be around a million by then. Compound interest is indeed the eighth wonder of the world!

You have already experienced this principle from building your current wealth, so you know what I am saying is true—the math does not lie.

Whatever you decide to give, put it in a trust or other financial instrument that will mature over decades. Yes, it will cost a few thousand to several thousand dollars to set up this trust. The good news? The main driver of increased costs (both to set up and to manage the trust over time) is complexity. Your trust is not complex. You are just adding money into index funds (like the S&P 500) and disbursement far in the future at a time (or times) that you set up in the trust.

Full disclosure: I have not done this yet. But I have been researching it with my accountant and estate planner, and it looks doable. Regardless of the set-up and ongoing costs, it will yield far more money (and *good*) to generations from now than by directly giving it to charity or the next generation of offspring only.

"But I love my kids too!"

Of course! This does not have to be a large sum of money, and most of your wealth can still go to your children or direct heirs. However, that trust will relieve them (assuming it is for grandkids, etc.) from having to save a significant amount for their children (your grandchildren).

Trust me (pun intended again): Funding your grandkids' education or retirement this way will save your children a fortune!

Part Four

Bringing it All Together

Conclusion

The purpose of this book was simple. It was to give you a basic, sound plan to achieve your financial success. It is based on my real-world experiences that led me to accomplish this goal myself. The book was never designed, nor is any other book intended, to be the only one you should read. Part of transforming yourself into what you want to become is discipline.

The root word is disciple, which simply means someone dedicated to a cause or belief. You wish to learn and "practice what you preach" to achieve your goal of financial success. So, you will continue to learn about personal finance, making and saving money, and put it all into practice in reality. There are *thousands* of great books on every endeavor you wish to strive for. Dedicate yourself right now to achieving your financial success.

I promise, based on what I KNOW, that economic

success will free you to do so much more in your later life. No one wants to have to work forever, especially not at a job they no longer like (or never liked). This book, if you follow even *most* of it religiously, will get you to where you want to be—to your Financial Success.

Here is the condensed version of this book, in conclusion:

There are things to do and things to avoid to achieve financial independence. Remember, the more you do, the faster you will get there...

Did you flip to the back of this book just to read this part? Awesome! Take the information below for free and run with it!

Hopefully, this will entice you to get this book and read the whole thing. Good luck in your financial journey, regardless!

These four items are your first goals; you start now if you haven't already:

• Get into a higher-paying job/career (this takes years to achieve in most cases)
• Stay out of, or at least limit, debt
• Avoid lifestyle creep
•Avoid, or at least plan for, expensive life events
• Invest at least one percent of each paycheck into your 401(k), and never stop as long as you have earned income

. . .

Once these five items are followed, and as you have more income and/or less expenses:

• Keep increasing the deductions going to that 401(k) until it is maxed out, and then keep doing it

• Once your 401(k) is maxed, start paying some into a Roth IRA as well

• Then max out your Roth IRA

• Then add in additional investments (if desired)

That's it. Pretty straightforward—and damn tough to actually do!

Things to speed up your investments and achieve financial independence earlier:

• Avoid expensive hobbies, or at least plan major purchases for them carefully.

• Kids, marriage (most include a later divorce), and "luxury" goods (cars, boats, planes, etc.) Avoid or plan for these significant (and expensive) things.

• Lifestyle items (clothes, jewelry, appearances)—avoid or limit these purchases; use this money to invest! Buying good-quality items as needed is one thing, but don't pay for "high fashion".

• Reflect carefully on where your money is going. The larger the sum, the more reflection you should engage in! In fact, buy a latte and ponder it...

I hope you have enjoyed this book and that it encourages you to increase your net worth over time. Being financially independent in your lifetime is achievable.

Also, it would be wonderful to hear from you, not only about this book and how it helped you, but also about making future ones. I love hearing that I helped someone improve their life! We all only live once, and our contributions to society and each other are among our most important legacies. My best wishes for your wealth and happiness!

Go for it!

Acknowledgments

I would like to thank all of the people who have helped me learn about finances, from conversations to books and teachers.

Also, I would like to thank the many others who have written on this important subject. Please consider reading some of the books I have listed in the appendix at the back of this book.

To my alpha and beta readers and editors, thank you.

Most importantly, I want to thank **you**, my reader.

Without readers such as yourself supporting authors, there would be few books to read at all ...

I look forward to hearing about your financial journey and am thankful I could be a small part in helping you with it.

About the Author

RK Jack is a retired government agent with over thirty years of experience in federal law enforcement and the military. He has been on SRT and VIPR teams and worked in uniformed and undercover positions, including twenty years as a federal air marshal (FAM). Before joining the civilian federal government, he deployed for OP Desert Storm as an enlisted soldier and later became a US Army National Guard lieutenant. He has been an instructor, both adjunct and full-time, for the government since the beginning of his service. This has given him a dedication to teach and impart knowledge to others in many fields of study.

His path is not the "traditional" route to financial security envisioned by most.

As a young man, he studied economics at the University of Colorado, Denver, until he figured out there was not much money to be made as an economist—this fueled his thirst for more financial knowledge. Using direct examples and life lessons, he shows the journey to financial independence through the lens of someone who has lived it. Over three decades of his working "career" life, he came to an understanding of the things he did well—and the things he did poorly—to build his financial wealth.

Public schools do not offer in-depth classes on personal wealth transformation. This is unfortunate, as the lessons we learn should be taught at a young age, not discovered "the hard way" as we go about our lives.

Financial literacy should be taught in grade school!

In this book, he categorizes and examines his life so that it may be shared with others. It is intended to help you learn what to do and not do on **your** path to Financial Success!

Connect with the Author

I hope you enjoyed reading my book!

If you would like to leave an honest review, it is always appreciated.

Sharing what I have learned has been ingrained in me from my many years as an instructor for soldiers, agents, law enforcement officers, and flight crews. I love teaching and sharing my knowledge, and in the process, I have learned so much from others as well.

If you would like to have me visit your book club or other group, I live in Denver, Colorado, and am available upon request. I can be reached anytime at my website at rkjackauthor.com

Thank you for your patronage!

Appendix

The following books were instrumental in my financial journey. Although far from an exhaustive list (there are a lot of good books out there), here are some of the ones that have had an impact on me:

The Debt Free and Prosperous Living—Basic Course©
   —John M. Commuta

Stocks for the Long Run©
   —Jeremy J. Siegel

Making Millions for Dummies©
   —Robert Doyen and Meg Schnieder

You Can Retire Sooner Than You Think©
   —Wes Moss

The Millionaire Mind©

—Thomas J. Stanley, Ph.D.

As always, I am continuing to learn and practice financial methodology. If you have recommendations, I would love to hear them!

Best of luck in *your* financial journey!

www.ingramcontent.com/pod-product-compliance
Lightning Source LLC
Chambersburg PA
CBHW070345130626
46556CB00007B/3036